Friends In High Places

By Mario Locatelli*

*The Montana Mountain Goat

Friends in High Places

By Mario Locatelli*

*The Montana Mountain Goat

Copyright 2015 by Mario Locatelli

ISBN 978-1-938707-17-9

Library of Congress Control Number 2015946701

Published in the United States of America

First Edition

STONEYDALE PRESS PUBLISHING COMPANY
523 Main Street • P.O. Box 188
Stevensville, Montana 59870
Phone: 406-777-2729
Email: stoneydale@stoneydale.com

DEDICATION

I wish to dedicate this book to two good friends who often accompanied me on trips into the high country, sometimes in the foulest of weather, to both enjoy that challenging environment and also to observe mountain goats in their natural habitat — George Corn and the late Steve Powell.

Cover Photo: *Friends in High Places, indeed! These are just some of the Mountain Goats that inspired Mario Locatelli, who is known to friends and admirers as the "Montana Mountain Goat," to produce this book featuring his encounters with these magnificent citizens of the high country. This mother and offspring nibble contently in Mario's presence while he photographed them just a hundred feet or so under the top of Montana's highest mountain, Granite Peak, 12,807 feet in elevation. Dozens of others he's met, often to the goat's surprise, occurred in a variety of Montana's high places, including his beloved Bitterroot Mountains near his home in western Montana. Naturally, he's photographed many of them and some are featured throughout the following pages – and it's easy to see why he is so captivated by the species. Please note that Mario has taken pictures of Mountain Goats over the past 40 years.*

Foreword

When it comes to commenting on denizens of the high country, few creatures have attained the respect and admiration among wildlife enthusiasts, or even the general public for that matter, that is held for the Rocky Mountain Goat, an admirable and noble species whose preference for living space is most often among the sheer cliffs and wildest of steep, wild country. Sure, you occasionally encounter mountain goats in gentle country, but not normally. They like, and generally inhabit, the places other species avoid: high, steep, barren, inhospitable, difficult and often icy, snow-covered country where, it seems, sheer idiocy reigns when it comes to moving about in the face of constant danger. And, sure, occasionally a mountain goat slips and plunges to his or her death in that high habitat, but only occasionally.

Those who observe them, and most often those observers, including me, are profound admirers of these critters. We marvel at their ability to negotiate the most precipitous of terrain, their seeming nimbleness afoot that constantly astounds us, and a hardiness that is basically incomprehensible. From their earliest days as kids, the mountain goat is faced daily with the reality that if it is to live in that high country, it must become as nimble afoot and nonchalant in attitude as its kin, and be willing to face the harshest of mountain terrain and climate. But, after all, these high places are theirs. It is their country, their abode, their dwelling place in a landscape that can be harsh but is, to them, a sanctuary from what must seem, a humdrum existence in less challenging land. It's a harsh life they lead, but a noble one. No wonder we admire them so.

Which brings us to the theme of this book – author and photographer Mario Locatelli's depiction of his relationship to the magnificent creatures we call mountain goats: friends in high places, indeed! This book might well be labeled an essay about an ingrained love and respect for this marvelous animal but, in reality it is more than that. This is a story laid out in front of us in text and photograph that shows us an intimacy with the mountain goat *and* its wild country. Take a good look at the photographs Mario has chosen to share with us! Mario has not only put himself in the high places where mountain goats are found; often, he's gone higher. And, as some photographs reveal, into steeper, more difficult terrain so he can get close in, above the unsuspecting subjects of his camera. Make special note to look for, in the eyes of some of his subjects in photographs spread throughout the following pages, for the element of surprise as the goats suddenly realize that some one, some thing, has gotten the drop on them. Wild as they are, supreme as they might be on the face of those cliffs, Mario has taken on their very nature to enable himself to move about *among them* in that high terrain. The result is a collection of photographs that enable us to share with him that insight into this amazing species. It is, for Mario, a personal relationship!

Now, we must also acknowledge in making this observation that, because of his lifetime of exploits of endurance and passion for the world's high places, Mario Locatelli has come to be known among the climbing community and the general public as "The Montana Mountain Goat." It's a fitting appellation. Not only has he conducted – repeat, conducted, been involved in personally, not just orchestrated – marathons of high country adventure but he's spent a good portion of his life traveling to and climbing the highest mountains in the world, including such places as Mount McKinley (Denali) in Alaska – indeed, he has climbed 50 of the highest mountains in the United States, as well as Kilimanjaro in Africa. Now into his early eighties, Mario Locatelli is a man of high energy who has insisted throughout his lifetime that what he sees and enjoys in the high places of the world is to be shared with others. He is, for example, also the author of *"The Mountain Goat Chronicles,"* his life story, and *"Hiking With Mario In Montana's Bitterroot Mountains,"* a guidebook. This book – *"Friends In High Places"* – is an effort to bring us into his world.. In it, Mario shares not only the joys of encountering his friends in high places but gives us, in his photographic observations, a real sense of the passion, and exertion, that enabled him to go up there, to those high places, and meet on equal terms the friends he found there. It was, and is, for us, a remarkable journey.

Dale A. Burk
Stevensville, Montana
July 20, 2015

Table of Contents

Chapter One

My Friends in High Places

The Rocky Mountain Goat is one of our most admirable, sought-after big game animals. His horns are not magnificent nor does his meat attract a gourmet, but his full white coat is beautiful and the fact that he lives in some of the most scenic country left on the face of this earth makes him special.

There are many factors affecting the survival of Mountain Goats. Right after the kids are born, an eagle has the strength to lift and carry them off. Eagles can also knock the kids and sub-adults off the cliffs. I've seen it happen and regret that I couldn't get a photo. Cold and rainy weather also affects the survival of a kid during the first weeks of its life.

The mating season is November and December and the kids are born in May and June.

Predators of the mountain goat are coyotes, cougar (mountain lions), bobcats, wolves, and golden and bald eagles.

Mountain Goats are known for being very agile but the rugged country

Getting higher than the Mountain Goats even in the rugged terrain where they are usually found is a good way to see them up close.

9

Goat country is generally in the high elevation areas. This scene shows the Bitterroot Valley in western Montana, where the author lives, far below the goat's regular living space.

they live in is difficult with the changing weather. Snow slides are also responsible for some of the deaths. The overhanging cornices have given way under the animal's weight, causing them to fall several hundred feet below. Sometimes Goats start a slide, because they feed and move across steep slopes and don't usually pay attention to the noise or movement of rolling rocks.

The Goat's diet consists of mountain grasses and once the snow is too deep they eat on shrubs and lower branches of trees. They also lick the rocks under the cliffs for the minerals they provide. When hiking and climbing Granite Peak in southwestern Montana, the highest mountain in Montana at 12,708 feet elevation, I stopped to relieve my bladder at the section called "The Froze to Death Plateau." The Goats enjoyed cleaning up after me; perhaps they liked the salt. With so many hikers on the mountain, they also seemed comfortable with the presence of humans.

Fighting is responsible for injury or death for many Mountain Goats, mainly the males. There is no doubt that serious wounds result between two males fighting during the rutting season. Severe climate conditions also are often responsible for heavy losses. Also, heavy snow depths can limit access to forage, so lack of food is sometimes fatal for them.

Once I spotted a female Goat on the edge of a cliff. I got so close to her that I could almost touch her, but she didn't seem to fear me. She couldn't get around me because I blocked her path. I then had to back up a few feet so I could get the entire goat in the photo. It's best to approach the Goats from above them; they seem to expect danger to be below and not above them. Sometimes when I try to get close to the Goats, they would stomp their feet to scare me away. When a Goat spots me, I get on all fours like I'm an animal and pretend to be foraging for food as well, scratching the ground with my hands. They don't pay as much attention to me then and go on feeding.

They can be very curious. One time I spotted several goats at a distance. I hid behind a rock so that I could reload my camera with film. I wasn't as sneaky as I thought because when I looked up to take pictures there was a young Billy about ten feet from me. I could barely get him in my lens frame. By the way, I took most of my photos of Mountain Goats with a Pentax 80x200 zoom lens.

The females are very protective of the kids. Once I saw an eagle flying toward a kid and the female ran toward the eagle to scare it away.

I've really enjoyed photographing Mountain Goats. I prefer this much more than hunting. They are the only big game animal that lives at such a

Typical Mountain Goat terrain. Often the temperature on my treks to the high goat country was between 10 above and 5 below zero.

high elevation, generally living between 4,000 to 9,000 feet above sea level. However, the higher elevations don't offer much food, so the Goats prefer to live on the south slopes because the snow and weather is not as severe as it is on the north side of the mountains.

For those who hunt the Mountain Goat, I have this advice: When hunting the Goats, avoid taking a female, particularly if accompanied by young kids. Kids stand little chance of survival after losing their mother. Make an effort to get a male. Carry binoculars to help identify between males and females. A male has a bigger chest and the horns are thicker. A big male has horns 10-11 inches long. They grow evenly from the base toward the back of the horns. The female's horns are thinner and go about three-quarters of the way before they make a turn toward the back of the Goat.

In 1995 my wife obtained a Goat permit and we hiked one of the westside canyons in the Bitterroot Mountains with my youngest daughter, Carmella. My wife bagged a nice Billy with a rifle that day. Through the years I've received two Goat permits and I bagged them both with my longbow. The best time to hunt Mountain Goats is toward the end of the season when the pelts are of much better quality. However, the Goats are harder to hunt at that time because of snow and ice on the cliffs, which makes your travel there treacherous. I've found that using crampons helps tremendously under such conditions.

Chapter Two

Editor's Note: *Over the years, Mario Locatelli has photographed Mountain Goats in a variety of high country terrain across the state of Montana. The following pages depict a selection of his favorite encounters with them.*

How close can you get to a wild Mountain Goat to take its picture? Quite close, actually! Here's a curious one the author met in the Bitterroot Mountains in western Montana who seems to want to know what that fellow with the Pentax camera is up to. Mario's response was that he considered it a joy to get up that close to the goat.

Two scenes that show the author's companions on many of his treks into the high country of the Selway-Bitterroot Wilderness in western Montana, where Mountain Goats find the sort of habitat they need to thrive. George Corn is in the photo at the top of the page and the late Steve Powell in the photo below.

Sometimes it was hard to spot goats due to the ice and snow on the mountains – and often you had to get quite close to see them.

Sometimes it is dangerous to climb up the mountainsides to see the goats up close, particularly for a person without any climbing experience.

I took these photos at 5 below zero.

I captured this picture of a wide-eyed goat looking at me close-up and she could not get away because I was blocking her escape route.

It was always an awesome experience to be able to get so close to the goats.

A couple of yearling mountain goats.

When spring-time comes around, they all start rubbing off their heavy winter coats.

Often the goats would hang on these sort of steep cliffs for hours and lick the minerals found on the rocks.

I found these goats to be very curious.

When the weather gets very stormy, they often hide under the rocky over-hangs and wait out the storm.

These two goats are about three to four months old.

I took these pictures in the spring.

Sometimes it is hard to get in close, so I had to take these pictures from a distance.

This is a nanny with her kid.

The goats are beautiful animals, always alert.

She is taking a rest, right out in the open.

The photo at the top is of a full-grown nanny. Below is a two-year-od billy.

Three goats taking a break.

"I caught you with my camera," I said to the goats in the photo at the top. Below, a young billy looked very surprised when I startled him by getting so close to him.

Four goats resting. They did not know I was there.

I had to hike up some 3,000 feet to get these pictures on the mountains on the west side of the Bitterroot Valley.

A young billy in the top photo, a young nanny in the picture below.

I killed two birds with one stone in getting these photos – good exercise and good pictures.

This goat played peek-a-boo with me.

On a very windy day, I captured this picture of beautiful goat.

41

Two nannies who obviously knew I was there.

In the spring and summer times, mountain goats find plenty to eat, so they fatten up for the harsh weather of winter.

The photo above was a very close-in shot of a young billy looking directly at me. Below we see a young nanny.

A couple of young billies.

Two billies.

I took these summer-time pictures of a magnificent goat on a lush hillside at Fred Burr Canyon on the west side of the Bitterroot Valley.

Enjoying themselves .. just browsing along.

Laying on an outcropping of this cliff, just enjoying the sunshine.

49

An adult nanny with her kid.

In the winter, the goats have a hard time finding food.

From a distance in the top photo, we find a goat resting on a snowbank. Below, another goat gives me a direct stare from close range.

It is amazing how sure-footed the goats are on this sort of difficult terrain.

Goats resting on snow-covered rocks are often hard to spot. Below, this goat looks very contented.

Two young billies looking right at me.

Two inquisitive young goats.

Two adult nannies.

It was awesome to get these pictures so close in to these goats standing on the edge of a cliff.

Hello there!

An adult billy climbing up the edge of a cliff.

On a cold winter day, they don't seem to mind the cold or the snow.

When looking at these pictures, one wonders how the goats can survive the winter in their alpine home.

A couple of billies on an icy abode in the top photo and a young kid on a rock below.

A nanny with her kid in the top photo, a young billy in the photo below.

Two young billies in very different terrain.

How nice it was to catch this goat looking at me from close range.

Two nannies with their kids.

Their hooves enable them to move on the steep slopes without slipping.

It is alleged that Mario has developed the ability to communicate directly with mountain goats because of his long association with them. This sequence of photographs seems to bear that out. First, he told this goat (upper left photo) to "Look right!" Then he said, "Look left!" And, finally, the word was, "Look directly into the camera." Enough said!

Home and Family

This high elevation and very old tree in goat country shows signs of being whipped by the wind day in and day out over a long period of time.

The author built his own home on his ranch on the west side of Bitterroot Valley, a stone's throw from where he's done most of his goat watching. These pictures show his place during the early phase of its construction.

This is a picture of me with my second daughter, Carlin, taken on our ranch.

This photo shows my youngest daughter, Carmella, at the right, and three of our grandchildren.

Mario (above photo) with four of his daughters and two grandchildren. Below with daughter Peggy at her gradution from Corvallis High School.

Photo above is of Mario's daughter Carlene. Below are daughters Peggy (left) and Angela.

Daughter Angela (above photo) on an elk hunting trip to the Gardiner, Montana, area. Below is daughter Carlene on a hillside overlooking the Bear Creek drainage of the Bitterroot Mountains near Mario's home just to the north of Hamilton, Montana.

My ex-wife and daughter Carmella on hunting trip years ago into the Bitterroot Mountains.

Here we're shown on an outcropping after the goat was bagged.

These are the sort of cliffs where the mountain goats are found.

Above photo is with the trophy. Bottom photo shows us heading home with the prize.

Chapter Four

Mountain Goats In Montana

A request to the Montana Department of Fish, Wildlife and Parks for information about the presence of Mountain Goats in Montana provided some valuable information that I pass on in this section of the book – with thanks to them for both the detailed information and the illustrating sketches.

First, the Mountain Goat (*Oreamnos americanus*) is the only genus and species of its kind in the world. Its closest relatives are the chamois of Europe and the goral and serow of Asia. The domestic goat is not closely related to the mountain goat.

Mountain goats occur only in northwestern North America. In Montana, they are native west of the Continental Divide and have been introduced into several mountain ranges east of the Divide.

Although goats do not typically venture far from cliffs and broken terrain, which provide escape cover from predators, they do use dense timber and creek bottoms for security and thermal cover against extreme heat, cold and wind. Within their range, mountain goats may be found at any

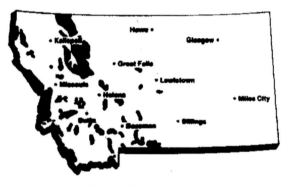

Mountain Goat distribution in Montana.

elevation or exposure at any time of the year. Some goats move down in winter to steep cliffs with good snow shedding properties, while others move up to wind-swept ridges to feed on exposed forage.

At birth, kids stand about 13 inches (34 cm.) at the shoulder and weigh five to 7 pounds (3 kg.) Yearlings may average about 45 pounds (20 kg.) And two-year-olds about 55 pounds (25 kg.). Mountain goats continue to grow through their fourth year, achieving average weights of 125 to 155 pounds (57 to 83 kg.) for females and 135 to 180 pounds (62 to 83 kg.) for males.

The breeding season occurs from mid-November through early December. Females do not breed until they're two and a half years old.

After a gestation period of six months, kids are born in late May or early June. Kids closely follow their mothers for the first year, relying upon them to expose winter forage in deep snow conditions.

Adult females rank highest in the social order. By association, kids also assume the superior status of their mothers, who vigorously defend them until the kids are one year old. Yearlings drop to the bottom of the pecking order and are forced to forage last in areas pawed out by other goats.

Kid and yearling survival may be less than 50 percent, depending upon the severity of the winter. Mountain goats have one of the highest natural mortality rates among big game animals due to the dangerous terrain and hostile climate in which they live and if a goat survives the juvenile years, longevity is normally 10 to 13 years.

Juvenile mountain goats learn a number of lessons from adult females, among them:
• How to safely use their range.
• How to move from one precipitous cliff dwelling to another.
• Where strategic feeding and bedding sites occur.
• When to make seasonal migrations.
• How to safely approach mineral licks, which may be removed from escape terrain.
• Where to find shelter in a storm.
• Where to cross snow-laden slopes.

In addition to maintaining the herd through offspring production, adult females are reservoirs of tradition and knowledge. Thus, the loss of an adult female from the population constitutes more than simply the loss of a single mountain goat.

Group Composition

Female-juvenile groups, also called "nursery groups," may range in size from two to well over a dozen mountain goats in native populations on the west side of the Continental Divide. In some introduced populations east of the Divide, groups of up to 50 goats sometimes can be observed. Large groups generally occur during early summer when goats congregate on prime feeding grounds or on mineral licks.

As the summer progresses and the vegetation dries out, group size diminishes. Although the juveniles are normally found in the company of adult females, a goat of any age or sex may be alone and careful scrutiny is required to determine its status.

By the age of two, males begin to disassociate themselves from the nursery groups. Adult males generally lead solitary lives and outside of the mating season they tend to associate primarily with other males. Females normally inhabit the most desirable cliffs, which are also often more visible and accessible than areas frequented by males. From late October to mid-December, males seek out females, so both sexes can be found together at this time of the year.

Pelage

Composed of a fine, thick underlay of very soft fur and an outer, longer, layer of guard hairs, the white coat of the Mountain Goat is one of the most beautiful of North American wildlife. Among hooved mammals, only the Dall Sheep shares the distinction of a pure white cape.

This coat is shed annually in the summer, but by November it has nearly reached its maximum length. Average maximum length of guard hairs on portions of the body is six to eight inches (15 to 20 cm.). Males tend to have more pronounced development of the beard and pantaloons and longer hair over the top of the shoulders than do females.

By late October, the Mountain Goat's beard becomes a reliable but subtle indicator of age. The adult's full beard extends the full length of the face and may reach six to seven inches (15.5 to 18 cm.) in length, while younger goats have progressively shorter, thinner beards. The full beard of an adult gives the face a wider appearance. In comparison, a yearling's beard seems to be confined to the chin and is less than four inches (10cm.) in length.

Males characteristically dig rutting pits as the breeding season approaches. Pawing the ground until a depression is created, the male will

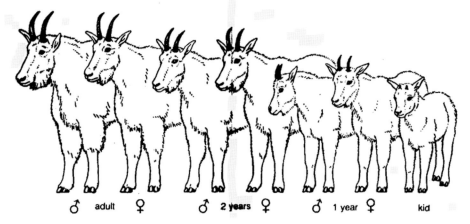

♂ adult ♀   ♂ 2 years ♀   ♂ 1 year ♀   kid

Comparison of Mountain Goats by sex and ages. Illustration courtesy FWP.

83

urinate in the pit and then lay in the moist dirt, often throwing loosened soil backwards with the front feet, over the flanks. This process results in a soiled coat, particularly around the knees and flanks. Females occasionally will in indulge in similar behavior, so a dirty coat is not a foolproof indication of a goat's sex.

Body Size and Configuration

Body size differences between male and female goats three years of age and younger cannot be reliable distinguished. In goats four years of age and older, males are usually larger than females, standing three to six inches (7.5 to 15 cm.) higher at the shoulder and slightly longer in body length.

Muscular development of the males' shoulders and the depth of the chest is greater than that of females. Subtle facial features may include a more angular appearance in males, although one- and two-year-olds retain a blocky appearance due to the shorter snout typical of juveniles.

Urination Posture

Probably the best feature in determining the sex of a Mountain Goat you encounter is its urination posture. The male stretches forward with the front legs to urinate, while keeping the hind legs stationary. The female stands in place, sometimes moving the hind legs apart, then squats to situate her rump closer to the ground.

At close range, when goats are still in summer pelage, the genitalia may be observed. By autumn, however, the winter coat generally obscures the scrotum of the male, but the black vulval patch of the female is visible when the tail is raised, regardless of the coat length.

Urination posture (left) for females and (right) for males. Illustration courtesy FWP.

Horns

Males and females both have shiny, black horns which grow from a bony core. Mountain Goats do not shed their horns.

An increment of growth is added to the horn annually. During the first year of life, the horns continue to grow throughout the winter so a distinct ring is not created, although a ridge or indentation in the horn often occurs. The majority of horn growth occurs during the first two and one-half years of the goat's life. The age of a goat may be determined by counting the annual growth rings on the horn, which are formed each winter except the first year. For example, the horns of a five-year-old goat, in the fall, will show four visible rings.

The male's horns curve back in a greater, more uniform arc than those of the female. The female's horns tend to curve more toward the tip, although this feature is variable

Average horn lengths for adult males range from eight to ten inches (20.3 to 25.4 cm.) and for adult females from 7.5 to 10 inches (19.0 to 25.4 cm.), depending on the area where they live. Although the lengths of a male's horns may not exceed those of a female, the circumference of the horns at the base is greater. A careful observer will notice that there is less space between the horns of males than females. Basal horn circumference for males ranges from 4.3 to 5.8 inches (1.7 to2.3 cm.) while in females circumference is from 3.5 to 5.0 inches (8.9 to 12.7 cm.)

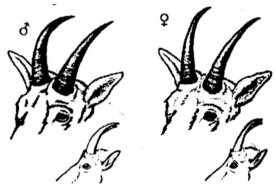

Female goat horns (right) and male horns (left). Illustration courtesy FWP.

Length of the horn in relation to the ear is a major key when trying to make a judgment in the field of the age of a Mountain Goat. From the age of one year, the ears are at least four inches (10.2 cm.) long, reaching 5.5 inches (14 cm.) in some adult males. In yearlings, the horns are equal or less than the length of the ear. In two-year-olds, the horns exceed the ear length by one to two inches, or up to half again the length of the ear. The horn-to-ear length ratio in adults is variable, but the horns are at least half again as long as the ears, and they may achieve double the length of the ears. If the horns appear to be full-length, but the nose seems short, the goat is probably a two- to three-year-old.

ALSO AVAILABLE

Additonal copies of *"Friends In High Places"* or Mario's other books are available by contacting the author at the address or phone number listed below. Information on cost and shipping charges is listed for each title:

MARIO LOCATELLI
165 Mountain Goat Road
Hamilton, Montana 59840
Phone: 406-363-1262

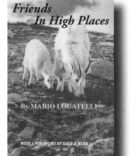

FRIENDS IN HIGH PLACES
$12.95 plus $3.00 shipping

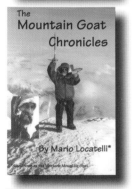

THE MOUNTAIN GOAT CHRONICLES
$12.95 plus $3.00 shipping

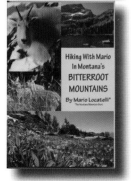

HIKING WITH MARIO IN MONTANA'S BITTERROOT MOUNTAINS
$14.95 plus $3.50 shipping